THE ACCIDENTAL

CANTO MUNDO
POETRY SERIES
EDITED BY DEBORAH PAREDEZ
AND CARMEN GIMÉNEZ SMITH

THE ACCIDENTAL

POEMS BY
GINA FRANCO

The University of Arkansas Press
Fayetteville
2019

Manufactured in the United States of America

ISBN: 978-1-68226-105-7
eISBN: 978-1-61075-675-4

23 22 21 20 19 5 4 3 2 1

Designed by Liz Lester

♾ The paper used in this publication meets the minimum requirements of the American National Standard for Permanence of Paper for Printed Library Materials Z39.48-1984.

Library of Congress Cataloging-in-Publication Data

Names: Franco, Gina L., author.
Title: The accidental / poems by Gina Franco.
Description: Fayetteville : The University of Arkansas Press, 2019. |
Identifiers: LCCN 2019000978 (print) | LCCN 2019003007 (ebook) | ISBN 9781610756754 (electronic) | ISBN 9781682261057 (pbk. : alk. paper)
Classification: LCC PS3606.R375 (ebook) | LCC PS3606.R375 A6 2019 (print) | DDC 811/.6--dc23
LC record available at https://lccn.loc.gov/2019000978

for Christopher
and for Sylvia and Dan
and Christopher

But it is prepared for us on dead wood, geometrically squared, where a corpse is hanging.

—SIMONE WEIL

At times, along this road with no edges, it seemed like there'd be nothing afterward, that nothing could be found on the other side, at the end of this plain split with cracks and dry arroyos. But there is something. There's a town.

—JUAN RULFO

SERIES EDITORS' PREFACE

Gina Franco's poems are bone and bark and bough; they are spirit and *sangre* and sutures for the wounds that dwell along the geographical and metaphysical space of the borderlands. Her work inhabits the darkness and the light of insight that breaks its seal: "Nevertheless, sobbing, hers, late and in the dark, while I lie awake and listen for a sign of something more." The speaker in her poems not only bears witness to the acts of racial and gendered injustice that mark her world, but she cries out with the purpose and propulsion of a *griot*: "I reflected," she writes, "I put my hands together; I kept on calling."

The poems in this collection excavate the histories of violence and endurance in the borderlands—in both the US-Mexico region from which the author hails and in the liminal spaces of struggle and searching that shape the lives in so many Latinx communities we call home. "& the wall crossed them all," she reminds us. For her, borders are marked not simply by irreparable loss and separation but by what remains, even if it is only a memory of what has been taken from us: "the remainder, the little peace which is / utterly / in want / [—of the other / side—] of / likeness, / the piece that goes missing, that remains / [the corpse of] / an absence." Franco's work dwells in the borderlands as a site of mourning and of resistance and, above all, of meaning-making and self-making. The border, as the long tradition of Latinx poets has reminded us, is *nepantla*, is a meta/physical location and psychic condition in which we struggle and from which we can emerge to enact political and aesthetic revolutions. Franco's book and its attention to "the other / side—]" is of utmost urgency in this moment marked by increased assaults against Latinx communities who are falsely and virulently positioned as a national emergency in the borderlands. As such, this collection is a fitting recipient of the 2019 CantoMundo Poetry Prize.

Since our founding in 2009 by a collective of cross-generational Latinx poets—Norma E. Cantú, Celeste Guzman Mendoza, Pablo Miguel Martínez, Deborah Paredez, and Carmen Tafolla—CantoMundo has sought to provide a space for the creation of Latinx poetry and a community of support for Latinx poets. Central to CantoMundo's mission is the desire to create opportunities—both within and beyond established institutions—for the development, documentation, performance, and publication of Latinx poetry: a *canto-mundo*, a world of song, sustained by the wide-ranging voices of Latinx poets. The CantoMundo Poetry Series arises out of CantoMundo's efforts to support and showcase Latinx poets from across the linguistic, aesthetic, stylistic, and cultural spectrums in which they write. The series values the traditions and communities from which contemporary Latinx poets emerge while also encouraging an engagement with innovative Latinx aesthetics and poetics.

Franco asks, "What did you learn from the dead?" The poems collected here take on, implicitly and explicitly, this sense of searching, this commitment to spiritual and philosophical meditation. Here the spirit is made flesh, and blood and bone are made holy. About Franco's collection, Emmy Pérez, this year's guest judge, observes:

> These extraordinary poems document a consciousness of being, in *nepantla*, where the narrator's abiding love for family and humanity unfurls in inquiry from estrangement, loss, and witness. Franco's gift is in philosophizing memory and the present, in creating multiple, intersecting worlds that span time and geographies. The work is a reminder that many of us who live away from where we were raised remain deeply connected to the land and memories of loved ones despite circumstances that would separate us. I cried out loud when I finished reading the book.

Franco's poems move through the borderlands between narrative and lyric, between startling enjambment and breathless lines, between that which keeps us earthbound and that which unfetters the soul: "Would that I could bring the body down, beneath the slow winter wasps and the tree withstanding its mutilations. Between the late sun, thief of shadows, and the morning sun, for whom the river would not part. I would say fall on us, green mountains. I would say cover us, green hills." We move with her beneath and between and across these exterior and interior landscapes; we move with her to, as Pérez did, release, at last, our own *gritos*.

Deborah Paredez and Carmen Giménez Smith

ACKNOWLEDGMENTS

Grateful acknowledgement is made to the editors of the following publications in which these poems, or variations of these poems, first appeared:

32 Poems, "The Stone is Worldless"; *Black Warrior Review,* "The Spirit Is Blood from a Stone"; *Blue Collar Review,* "The Line"*;* *BorderSenses,* from "The Accidental"; *Copper Nickel,* from "The Accidental"*;* *Crazyhorse,* "The Animal Is Poor in the World," "Water in Water"; *The Delaware Review,* from "Substantial"; *Diagram,* "Otherwise All Would Be God"; *Drunken Boat,* from "The Accidental"; *The Eleventh Muse,* from "Substantial"; *Fence,* "The Box"; *Image,* "World-Making: Foundations of a Marvelous Science," "Litany for a Table of Immovable Feasts"; *MiPOesias,* "America"; *Narrative,* "Annunciation of the Self-Enclosed God"; *Pilgrimage,* "What Shall I Cry," "Our Mother of Rivers Is Made Our Perpetual Hanging Garden"; *Poetry,* "Refrain"; *Saint Katherine Review,* from "Substantial"; *Tuesday; an Art Project,* "The Wall"; *West Branch Wired,* "The Spirit Is Bone," from "Substantial," "Retablo:"; *Zócalo,* "Fiat"; *Zone 3,* from "The Accidental."

"The Box" also appeared in *A Best of Fence, The First Nine Years,* edited by Rebecca Wolff, Fence Books, 2009. "The Stone Is Worldless," "The Wall," and "The Spirit Is Blood from a Stone" were each nominated for a Pushcart Prize. "The Spirit Is Blood from a Stone" received a Pushcart Special Mention under the title, "The Earth Without." Many thanks to each of those editors for their nominations.

Thanks to the institutional support of faculty research at Knox College, particularly through the John and Elaine Fellowes Fund for English Literature and Writing, the Religious Studies Fund, and the Andrew W. Mellon Foundation. Thanks also to the Letras Latinas Literary Initiative of the Institute for Latino Studies at the University of Notre Dame, particularly to Francisco Aragón. Thanks to the Bread Loaf Writers' Conference for the 2006 Meralmikjen Fellowship in Poetry, which was instrumental to my art and faith. Thanks to the Brothers of St. John in Princeville, Illinois, for allowing me into their classrooms at the novitiate School of St. John, and to those monks who were my teachers and spiritual guides, especially Father John-Luke. Thanks, Casa Libre en la Solana of Tucson, Arizona, for providing a summer writing residency. Thanks, *Image* journal for the Glen Workshop at St. John's College in Santa Fe, New Mexico. Thanks to the series editors of the CantoMundo Poetry Prize, Celeste Guzmán Mendoza, Deborah Paredez, and Carmen Giménez Smith, and to Emmy Pérez, who selected the book. Thanks to everyone at the University of Arkansas Press, especially David Scott Cunningham, Melissa King, Liz Lester, and Molly Rector, and to Anthony Blake. Thanks to Frank Gaspar, reader and adviser, to Meg Files for her endless support and love, and to Stacy Poore for the summers at Big River Ranch at the little cabin of more than thirty-three trees in Creede, Colorado, where this book was completed. To Christopher and to all of our family: thank you. You are nothing less than essential.

CONTENTS

THE ACCIDENTAL

Otherwise All Would Be God

for Carmen Rios, flood victim, whose body was recovered from a tree, Del Rio, Texas, August 22, 1998

In an hour before now I began the book of annunciations, for then I knew nothing would arrive but wilderness. The wind was kicking up as I stood beneath the tree where the body had been. The limbs shuddered and had the look of things that had been touched, and had I not been afraid of myself that way, I would have knelt before their splendor. Though surely it is too late for invisible things to make an outcry, too late for one thing to arrive speaking as another, the wind kicking up, the wind (be still) blowing in one direction, plainly, just as, it seemed then, freedom had entered my life, adrift. No angel arose from the forking branches nor hissed from the dead leaves. The lot down the street where the mother's house stood is empty, and the memory of the grave (pane of punched tin, smooth furrow in the earth) is in the same way empty. I stood at the foot of the mesquite where the wind was kicking up and remembered you writing the last letter you would send: *I tried to call you, you know, but you weren't home, and before I left a message, I thought how invasive of me! and I hung up.* How does a call (where are you?) not end in expulsion, the mind (I am hiding) apportioned in all that body, the mind (I am naked) bending light to earth, the mind (I am shamed) trembling in its very last limbs?

SUBSTANTIAL

We must be careful about the level on which we place the infinite. If we place it on the level which is only suitable for the finite it will matter very little what name we give it.

—SIMONE WEIL

The Stone Is Worldless

being left empty by the refusal of things

Then dread seemed preferable to emptiness.
Like that feeling of watching the tree heave and wave
and fill with crows, their wings blackening the fog
in the branches, the tree teeming with handlike shadows
grasping for air. Their sudden departure. In which the tree
shivers now less meaningfully. No more a certainty at hand
that stalls and stalls and never arrives, but a static that is hard
to shake. Little upset bowl, little indoor storm (*when a sieve*
is shaken, refuse remains), the snow globe scattered its stars
over the clearing, and the deepest transparencies grew
faint, and this was a comfort until the flurry became
a frozen surface, same and same. Whether beneath it the tree
is throwing long bars of shadow across the churchyard
in the center, whether in the center the vaults loom up
and put themselves in order. If in the seeming of the vaults
there is an *in*, something deeper, that's a question
no different from the worst lonesomeness, empty
dwelling. The lost home. Interred somewhere, but where
is not the point of this world. Neither is trepidation,
the stone face saying: *What is stone and what is stone*
passing itself off as everything else are the same. In the end.
So endlessly, the unsettling parts. It is hard to look
away. While the snow makes a burial ground of the circle
of field. While the field ends where it meets the stream.
While the stream runs into the distance and the distance
curves back on itself, either like a refusal to give and give,
which is the expected thing, or like an indication of return,
your return, evidence that the tree is emptied for all
the reason of the shaking world.

Fiat

No iridescence, really, but a ruse
of oil, this white room and its angel.
Who walks in a wail of flame. Nothing
here bears color without pain.
Red gash, blue vein. The eye
is plunged by glut but sees more void,
and the mind stammers and the mind
doubts: *Love is a garment . . . love is a ghost . . .*
So that the pair is no pair, but one
rubbed from a dream. So that the mind
in its bed throws a mighty silhouette, so that
a halo eclipses the dark. So that one
overshadowed gazes into the future
of illusions. Is this death or is it life?
The denuded star. The said
God. The sapling tree in the background,
the longing in the window. And the window:
drawn wide open in a boom of light.
Sound to eye (total absence is a lie?),
the child-mother hunches by.

What Shall I Cry?

all flesh is grass

Nevertheless, sobbing, hers, late and in the dark, while I lie
awake and listen for a sign of something more.

Girl at the back stairs with her baby in her arms, baby being
buckled into the car. The top of his head a soft golden frizz,
his skin a deep baby brown. She buckles him lovingly in while
he sleeps and strokes his lolling head before shutting the door
on him, soundly.

Outside, a black moth flaps at the window, beats at the dark
interior of the glass where my face is. Withdraws, indecipherable.

On the one hand, a commotion in the lower left corner, a sigh
shuddering like love through the honeysuckle, and the bush burns
its bright dry leaves in the drought, offering what it is given.

On the other hand, a shadow takes over the grass. A bruise.

Which devoured one side of his face, and for weeks I felt my face
turn away.

The day mirrors in the sun. The sun glancing off low-flying planes.
The sun flaring through insect wings and blazing in the harvest
fields. The sun like a lit wick in the engine that grinds its ball
to dirt.

A she-dove all shades of ash mourns through the yard at noon
and scratches at the earth in thirst.

One night she slept in the car with the engine running, and for days
there was no baby.

On the one hand, a fist and tiny nails. On the other hand,
more nails.

I cannot say what the cry was like, if there were words in it,
or warbling, if mourning was all there was.

He's two going on three she says when they move in upstairs.
And he throws a hissy sometimes, her way of saying there will be
some crying.

Their droppings rain down from the eaves. Indiscernible
from the window, the doves gray the fruit trees, the oleanders.
The grass. Which I know without looking is dying in the corners
of the garden

whether or not I look after it. Eyeless as memory, the three-headed
bellows (boy, mother, and occasional father) bawl above me
and every night

again, the evangelist waves his glass eye at the congregation that
rushes the platform weeping for proof, and the God in the eye
says ask.

On the one hand, the glassblower worked his prayer
on the bellows, and the bellows flamed the fire, and the fire
melted glass, warmed the house, baked the bread,
and the remainder made a beautiful light by which to see,
and so the glassblower who was also a painter, painted.

In the crawl space between us, her broom scratches at the corners
of the attic and is amplified. A spatula scrapes a pan, a pan
the stove, a chair the floor. The baby kicks the walls and burbles
and screeches in the room above my head.

On the other hand, the sick roses blackened indoors. The starlings
bred in the porch rot that spring and the fall blew in swarms of red
beetles from the fields who stained the sills of the house with their
dead.

Hammering and hammering, the father makes sound work
of the son and the son, obedient, is silent.

The evangelist patches his one good eye and stares

into anonymity. In the dream of the transparent sign the wound
closes over the ball, and the ball housels there,

and the ball rolls presciently. Everywhere

in compositions Gabriel arrives with lilies. At times the girl-mother
is surprised in her bedroom and fixes her gaze on a spot in front
of her. At times the messenger's wings are on fire and the sun
pierces through the glass. At times, the angel wears a crown
in the garden enclosure. He speaks to her in gold leaf as she weighs
the book of hours, spread out, in her hands,

(on the one hand an eye, on the other hand an eye)

and a young tree spires in the square window, wordlessly,
and the sun is suspended, hanging in the sky.

(The voice says cry.)

Night from night heaves and divides, broods and multiplies,
so the darkness is pierced but not broken.

The police never arrive when I call.

The Animal Is Poor in the World

In the story, there was no moment of flight,
                    the flock startled, lifting at once, first light, still
stars, dark articles spreading into the utter reach
                    of the flock, the flock vanishing—without
grief—as if to disclose that the world ends in wanting
                    more world—;—no. In the story
the animals came, one by one, fowled or creeping
                    into the open, and each name given was like
a pane of clear glass. Like the window of my room
                    that looks out on the spire of the closed church,
the glass drawing the eye back to where the bird flew
                    against it, leaving a dust of wings and red down

[—;—]

in the story about spirit and meat at odds—isn't it odd—
                    the cardinal thing beat at the skull, seeing world inside,
world other side, world through, knocking itself out
                    because vision—stubborn vision—is always going
where the body can't follow. Pained with getting
                    up again, nonetheless it began: in the story I like,
whatever I called them is what they were called,
                    and applauding, meanwhile, the Lord in the story heard
what all was called and nodded in likeness, and because nothing
                    on earth like me was me but the names
of the creatures as they appeared in the clearing, I reflected;
                    I put my hands together; I kept on calling

The Line

a serious surplus population that needs eliminating

So now we are equals, verdad? All along eyeing the same banks,
as though we might surface on the same shore, bare backs
to the sun, wet shirts in hand, boots aside, those too.
You keep saying, *El otro lado*. See you there,
face to face, no worries.
The last good lynching
was long ago. Ropes, belts, canteens sway in the tree. The tree
sings with lightness. In time, the fruit shrank in the heat, grinned
wide from the bone, dropped to the dirt.
Rot. The earthworm's
heart, this now. A knot, a fishing spot.
The sweet-blood smell of the hook right through, the impaled
form, right through, either soft end writhing on the line.
Beneath the surface, neither vertebral nor articulate, it sways
under water—guts in skin—it sways from the other side, verdad,
not a lure but a rumor, a mirror, of a parallel end;

we'd fished the shallows with stripped willows,
with a hellgrammite drifting in the current,
and that's where we trapped our leviathan,
iridescent scales that slid away from our hands,
where we crossed the swinging bridge and found
effigy and sign, *Death to scabs crossing the line*,
a volleyball head and a pair of shovels for limbs,
the hanging white sheet, the slashed body of many:

the hanging white sheet, the slashed body of many:
a volleyball head and a pair of shovels for limbs,

effigy and sign, *Death to scabs crossing the line*,
where we crossed the swinging bridge and found
iridescent scales that slid away from our hands,
and that's where we trapped our leviathan,
with a hellgrammite drifting in the current,
we'd fished the shallows with stripped willows

y verdad, the cities on either side of the river watch
one another from the eyes of their televisions.
Their headlines race beneath glass

—they have taken my father's body
and I do not know where they have laid him—

and light. Love as the sinker, the line sinking deep. The last time
I saw my father was in a dream, seated on every side of the table
of ancestors, and belonging so fully, he ceased
        to exist. They arrived
on the other side, at the tree at the end of this world, and the tree
drank deeply. Love as a secret, unbearable map. Tell me—*verdad*—
where you have laid the body (and

I will bear
him away. I
will bear him a-
way. I will bear
him a way).

The Spirit Is Bone

From here
everything
outside is
invisible, all
but the view
[—a be
-lief—] through
the one open
window: the room's partial tree, leaf-
less yet: partial
stone-
hinged clouds
drifting
off, becoming
other clouds in the other
unseen sky
[where
the tree is
finished]. From
here one
-sided mind is
filling in.
From here
the recollections, the symmetries, the familiar
forms: vanished
stars: tiny
morning
[into which the end of the tree disappears]

And all
that trouble,

the remainder, the little peace which is

utterly
in want

[—of the other

side—] of
likeness,

the piece that goes missing, that remains

[the corpse of]
an absence,

a thing itself, [the ghost of]

a chance, from
here, begging

begging

the question—

Refrain

It would never be possible for a stone, any more than for an airplane, to elevate itself toward the sun in jubilation.

The dragonflies again; the last time seeing them
skim the river so close
                                        to forgotten—their singing,
their shimmer—now remembered, now becoming so much
flame;
          as tongues over the heads of the chosen
in the child's picture book of Christ I learned
by heart, here is descent and weight of after-
the-fact, the gift
                              the fork
between hope and vanity, and the river that eats
itself turned mirror broken into
                                                    light; the corpse
between the beloved's good word
and the beloved
                              who, having spoken, was ever spoken
into being lies, unspeaking, and as with any heaviness that lowers
then hovers, remains
                                        inconceivable; so the letter given in stone,
so perfection
in fire;
love; all
          love's failures; the winged animal

drops to the earth and is there buried in a hole where it digs
in the grit like the blade
                                                  we left in the riverbed, adrift and cry-
shaped in the memory, both
that dim and that loud; though
                                                                  no accosting why it
seems that way, everything ghost
of itself or everything made
                                                            of mythic proportion, the walker
sinking from the face of the waters, the dragon I
become when I talk to myself, what a belief
                                                                                    is, terrifying
and relentless; I've never been
able to tell the difference;
                                                      the brute and the apparition
in reflection speak at once—the rock and the rock's light—
so that now the insect thrums
                                                                and it is surely
a kind of tenderness, an ODing in secret, turning into while turning
from the soul that the animal raised
                                                                          and devoured in dream; imagine,
the child's wished-for surface gives and ripples up
                                                                                                to mouth

the perfect imprint, saying “aircraft” and there are aircraft, amen,
the walker is surrounded by flight on all sides;

                                                                                the walker

walks without wings; see,

the recollection is flawless, turning wings of jewels;
the recollection is absolute, swallows whole;

                                                                                echoes;

and the dragon feasts; and the dragon flies again;

America

for Maribel Alejandra Cortinas Segura, stabbed to death by Hermengildo Lomas, January 5, 2009, Del Rio, Texas

At first, I was alone, as when going home. The women I used to know were on the escalators as they had been before. I had maps in my hands, and at my feet, my long black bag rode with me past their blue and garish faces, their faces mauled, made up, their faces splayed in the surfaces, passing and not passing, where I repeat myself too.

Like you, I'd do.

The terminal went a long way out, so I began walking. I began talking to you, cousins. Someone has drawn you in soft black paint, fetish and leathered, outlined and packaged, against a wall, my cousins. Someone has left another body in the sand, human, sallow, hornless as a hunted animal, naked and socket-eyed.

Blades in the eyes. Gutted like you.

Back from where we came—from where we'd leave again—you break for the cities kept behind glass, the escalating windows filled with sun, the glass rivers cutting across the ever-middle americas, that side, that side, that side, that side, that jealous side, the sun in a glass box, the drowned sun and the drowned rising, eddying against banks. Towards the bank.

That followed you.

See the poppies light the sand. The hills are standing open with golden armloads in the dream of the photograph on the wall of my dream. In the negative every face is a stain—a lack of light, spreading—an outline lost to the seared-in flesh. In the negative, shifting rivers, shifting sun, neither mapped nor tramped, and their fire is precisely the same dark. Like that, the body in the sand longs to enter the frame before disappearing entirely.

Like you, not you.

The Box

What did you learn from the dead?
To turn cold in stages to damn an invisible
instant bleed to check to have not
bled out to not heart to sight red to get off your
chest to neck to stomach to blow it right
out of the hole hard to kiss to how does it go off how
does it go stone deaf to so cold to so—so we heard
them last night shriek at each other the bejeezus though nobody
hours heard the shots, you?
Past tense of shoot also called scattergun also a slug
of clear liquid an injection to interject. To check. You?
O I gave it a shot resolved my greatest desire means
to go home a marked entry an engraved—no stoned—
entry to how do
you sleep how do you recognize now a boxed entry I'll
do to you shotgun I mean hotshot I'll do sick
of you yeah then go I'm serious like you
care to miscalculate the command of the exit to wound to
miss to cross
-fire hair also revolve, er, volver, also vamoose
called ghost word yeah gimme our faker way to square
—to shut [past tense of shoot] off—to check ammo, ur-,
am-our: go now I'm
on site.

Substantial

[a love letter]

I thought if I could
put the dream down

facts would emerge

from the remains, bones
from liquefaction. Soul,

-

as much stomach
as you are stone.
A homesickness

-

bound for the light of things. The meadow

bogged with puddles of cloud and sky
that day. Rainwater everywhere

was a mirror. We could see no interior.
The crows followed from the rooftops, dived

at us, contemptuous, until maybe we walked out
on them. We could see no territory.

Dusk made us stick, at last, to the shoulder
of the road, single-

file against the onslaught of headlights:

-

the lip of the horizon, affliction,

-

the same depth as skin of a body—
all skin. I want you to exist

well past the obelisk between us. I, if

not solely. I keep saying *I cannot be you.*
One of us is distant and so we both are

-

the

obelisk with the life
of a jar, the obelisk

over the square, over

the grave houses
and street litter and

rock

-

and dirt road.
      Empty bottle. Road
-kill. The body

      rots in the heat
mirage. The bottle
      beads in the sun.

If there is
      a message: someone
once here is not

-

      too far gone

-

      in the distance. Cloud cover. Eight-legged
horse with opposing heads. The animal

      holds together till the hill

bends the road and tears one from kind by a scant
      pelt of light: a mare: another mare: night

-

      -fall: lamplight: tree
that empties in a mess
      of fog: I that empty in

your absence to another
of your books: whether
soul has parts or is

indivisible, if it exists
everywhere in
everything substantially

the same, and how
can it, given that will
or mind or sense

or sympathy might
be the very stuff
of it, meanwhile, also

tearing soul into past
and future loves, where
soul can't much live:

-

such is this book
[once tree, once roots
with leaves] I love,

-

like you a light

-

from old light,
        having being
from a more first

-

        knowing—hidden,
unearthed, hidden
        again—in many ways

-

very human
        in hope, another
pillar, looking back

-

        at loss, God
of the dead, God of the tree
        cut down

-

and stripped to nothing:

-

the obelisk, a staff
with a serpent

inside, the obelisk

full of place
to hide what's been lied

-

at length. The moon

opens a blank after all-night
crying. Morning, inexplicable

hush. The toy endlessly chiming in the attic

apartment above me has been
missing for weeks now. What became of

it? Fascination

wore off. It was lost, left behind, beloved
but taken away. It was hidden

from the child when I complained

about other people
and their noise. It was

[—the obelisk,

-

a radio tower blinking above the sounds of the dying

-

city—]

broken. Our father dies in our city, and the wound
is deafening. It mouths for the living what living repeats to outlive

death: mutilation; ruin; defacement; pain: there is the flash

against respirator, bruise, jaundiced eyes and skin, blood
and excrement; there is the horizon in plain view and it looks

impossible; there is our father in our father's agony; there is

involuntary decay; there, in the midst of the metropolis
of the body—waking, breakfasting, stepping through fish

in shallow water, taking photographs of the ones that struck

the sand that morning before the household
woke—I somehow move myself; and there is the elegy, sound,

in the mouth; and there is the ghost in the liver;

[—and

-

all other
sound is

senseless; all

other sound
is noise—]

-

and there is the you
beyond it, intact

somehow, the one who lives.
Noise has no theology. Really,
you ascend from its volumes

announcing yourself, as if
repeating what has just been
said. As if the beauty of

the repeatable is not
coincidence but sacrament,
the similar not same

but parallel, the same
being true for who, for who
paired is a

-

marriage; believe

-

    in
God, believe
    in

-

that kind of narrative. All that partiality of the said "I"—all

-

    in all. The years

I've lived here, rarely
have the neighbors been kind

    to the people they love.

Downstairs, the son is grown.
The man he is now threatens

    to beat his mother.

They will last that way. They have
loved that way a long time—

-

wary of everything.
Anger. No pity.
Which feels definite,
like knowing

-

better: nothing but
[noise and the illusion of]

music. Nothing but
[violence and the illusion of]

mercy. Nothing but
[hunger and the illusion of]

sacrifice. Nothing but
[chaos and the illusion of]

order
[the illusion of] emerging

-

in the clouds. Your face. Far from here.

It is the season for long shadows, shadows
that look like time yawning in the stony yard.

Crickets, no birds. The sun not yet past houses.

Shadows that look like the invisible rods
of the world are showing.
Are bearing their intimating weight.

Stalwart shadows. Weight, but no news.

Held together, there is the prison in view.
Held apart, the abandoned asylum.

But upheld, if so, it is all so beautiful. I thought

-

if I could put the dream down, the dream
would emerge absolved of all dream, all
dreaminess in it destroyed. The roses in

the courtyard garden have opened once more so far, so
extravagantly and with such excess, there is nothing
left for them but to winter, nakedly, in the bed of deadheads

and thorns, and so it goes with sacrifice. All
the agony, the needlessness, the stupid
pain surpassed, the victim arrives at the end

-

of itself, face
to face, nevermore
to be

treated as just
another matter:

-

infinite,

-

is it? Real silence?

That will endure, that won't raise its voice
in the square—where I thought I last saw

you—

against you. Music crossing the wind
-chimes, bells from a nearby

tower.

Vespers. Our favorite hour. And despite every
-thing you've been to me, how I know you will be

home.

Water in Water

a vision in which we see nothing

Where the darkness grew darkest it seemed
to deepen, to cave; thus, the light was light
in relief. I watched you climb to the top
of the hill, ascending the way memory or
ache will pierce through to the surface as all
else recedes into the deep. Us. Something
not-wind whispering the trees. A prominence
falling beneath you. The abandoned chain
factory with its row of windows observing
the gorge below as you rose into focus, and
the darkness made uncertain faces, and the fire
-light could no longer be seen. Why you tower
at the center of these dreams, why the dream
drains away, leaves you behind, solid, intact,
as nothing else is. The monolithic heart
of the machine that winds itself in iron. Into
perpetuity. Even once night has surely leveled
the proximities and the distances, the details,
the abstractions, the forms and silhouettes,
—the depths—of other manifestations
of being, and all is dark as sleep, it is an evening
in vain. There you are, oblivion. And ruin
doing what it does in the mind—the part that
remains laying waste to the part that died out
by filling in, linking together, at times tenderly,
faults to parts—ruin doing what it does by

finishing itself—I could hear the chains dragging
along the warehouse floor, along the heart
-walls of the factory where the machinery coils
the iron piles and the chain reels and reels
inside the sound of the gorge rushing with river.

Annunciation of the Self-Enclosed God

It is one thing to invoke the beloved, to have him
    stand at the door, armed with blossoms, and knock—
it's another to have him hesitate, silent, on the porch,

    pictured in the wide-angle lens that flattens him
and the house into the single dimension of a monochrome
    snapshot, a sameness in which the turret windows

stonewall over the gray porch, enclosing nothing, echoing
    nothing, though in reality the day is damp, hot, green, full
of orange insects in flight and the smell of mown dandelions

    and the squeal of the wood door that swells
with rain, that sticks in the jamb if one should be home to open
    it to the beloved, this unmoved beloved, who is

by now a figure of doubt

in a blue suit made bright by the yellow-house
    enormity around him, the beloved who stands
with his back to us, as if he will remain a stranger

    for ages—and given that he has become trivial, almost
minuscule, in the scene, given that he is less revelation
    than a longing-looking shadow among long morning shadows

—it's true;

it's likely he'll become the intruder in the silver world
          of the negative, however willingly; for once summoned,
what is left but to become a flash of angel, or ghost, a bar

          of time, motionless but about to move, not a who
who chose to enter the frame of this otherwise impersonal address,
          but an analogy, as it's been said, of the missing enclosure

of God,

the open fields of impressions, disfigurements, tricks
          of light, lies, all those stories within which the out-of-place
beloved, the unloved beloved, is turned away as unrecognizable,

          as a remnant left to leave the peonies on the door to wilt
in white paper (petals spoiling on the stoop) without, after all,
          knocking, and—given a frame or two—to turn

towards the open

street, to pause to notice that the mown grass
          has collected on his wingtips, to step briskly,
lightly, in a half flight down the few remaining

feet of walk belonging to the yellow house
with the set of white doors that become a backdrop for the pink
forsaken peonies, so that now what is left

is a beautiful frame with a beautiful object dying inside
it, left without inscription or signature, a photograph
in itself, pretty, but utterly messageless, which, in time,

does seem to be the fate of still life, that it says
so little, or that rarely it speaks without quoting itself—*Peonies,*
Door—over and over, with that self-enclosed

gaze that excludes any chance of the Thou coming
into the picture, the One arriving who so badly
wants to be spoken to, into, existence,

who wants

to have been awaited and wished for and begotten
for this end, who longs for this end to speak, to say,
at last, you,

you are

here, as a sign of what is significant, like a book
of hours laid open midday in outstretched hands, wearily,
on a day that has not yet given much thought

to hope and that is boxed in
by emptiness on every side, not unlike the scene recently
abandoned by the beloved, who, though

he chickened out, really, can hardly be blamed, since
it appears no one is home in the yellow house to look
out the turret windows from the desk, to have

seen the gardener—and landlord—give shape
to the bushes with his shears, weed the beds of stray morning
glories, water, rake up what he cut down, light

it on fire, and leave the garden pretty well near
perfect by the time the beautiful messenger appeared
in the frame with his gigantic flowering sea, one

arm dripping bright petals down to the stoop and his suit
the color of the right sky, though I may be confused with memory,
the time I watched from the lens of my camera

my colorful beloved throw flowers into the bay, watched his sea
of petals break and rise and eventually sink, quite another
thing from the failure we have seen in this unfinished art

-work, the annunciation

reduced to generalized taciturnity with expectation
that it may never speak again, if it ever spoke
previously, and is thus what seems left, often,

since the garden

expulsion: a dull pointlessness of things, this frame and this object
in the frame—pink flesh against wood; sagging heads
so heavy; leaves hardly outstretched anymore—

this simultaneous dying and blooming all too familiar
and, well, sad, too sad to keep looking, though mostly
we ignore what grieving comes of putting everything, me,

on exhibit, or—more true—of forgetting—and this
is the thing—that the grail holds absolutely nothing
if there is no beloved pouring his wine-sea into the overflowing

cup, if

he has so far withdrawn that he no longer exists
but as an image of longing: the man ascending the stairs
with an armful of Pentecost roses, the man in a hush

stepping out of his shoes to surprise his beloved, the man
and his beloved—who is surprised though not very—
standing together in the stairwell as his beloved slips her arms

around his middle and hugs her head against him, his
beloved who descended the stairs to say . . . *the vines have*
budded . . . the grape blossoms have

opened . . . and over our doors are all

choice fruits, new as well as old, which I have
laid up for thee, O my beloved.

The Spirit Is Thrown

existing, it never gets back behind its thrownness

[the rest of]
                the tree

behind

[the remains of]
                the tree

Retablo:

behind the altar

statue at the end of the world: statue wholly veil:
  a tiny tree is made
a house—as seen from beyond, omnisciently—with a wood

table placed inside to mark an opening: stretch of time
  between shape and meaning
of shape: this is

  [.]

body, covenant, a leaning into and a hush of thought as thought
  almost . . . almost
leans away, a lack of words, of dream, and a forgetting: the dream

of the wood is home and the dream of the home is where self
  does its looking into: every shelter is an image of
interiority: every book, the mind knows, is another word for tree:

are you there we wish so often: less intently where bread arrives
  before the table is set
in the hushed house: the wish of the altar is the image of the tree

in the wish of the carpenter: wooden cup, wooden plate,
  wooden table—as seen from behind, partially—
a petitioner's blindness: but also, devotion; this is

  [:]

corpus, our statue: every image is a book of judgments: measures
        taken apart from the whole given whole:
the image of the plate becomes the triumph of surface: landscape

without monument or aperture: blank face of the mirror: the image
        of the cup is bereavement
of depth: the hollowed body, more surface: more flesh of thought

        [. . .]

flesh: the wish of the altar is transfigured image: sky | star | tree
        . . . blue firmament | wormwood | rood . . .
the wish of the image is all it must bear: veil turned holy real:

Litany for a Table of Immovable Feasts

Stay for me, still life, ceaseless
tree, stay. Stay who stays
the real, you root of mind, you
constant mote. Pruned shoot, sealed
board, beam of sudden, come back
for me, please. Wood you. Say. For me, last
possible whole world, for wouldn't-me
still possible to believe, for place stay
put, for fruit in fool, for call against but,
meal against fell, guest within the rule
in will: you all me. You me me.
Who promised me. Who likened me, made
fetish me, and grieved me, but pleasure
me? Hunger me. Over-stander me.
Bored me, my act. Stay for me.
Come back to flee the rest of me,
to specter me and put an end
to me, to negative me through
and through. For I consume too much
of me, poor me, for my feel-possible you.

Our Mother of Rivers Is Made Our Perpetual Hanging Garden

The waters fell, the waters rose, and the eating places and the sleeping places of the city were carried into the streets where the rivers were singing as the living places gave way. There was the horizon, steeped in abjection and aching for nightfall, which felt like closure, inconceivable, but necessary. There was the tree in the bend of the road where—having followed the body's path to understand for myself—I watched the sun fade from the remains of the limbs. There, the limbs had caught the body up and held it fast against the flood. There, the wind tossed old leaves aside, exposing where the ash of the tree had split and wept. There was milk, rising into scars. Whatever was naked was unbearably naked, lanced clean through in a blink of an eye. And here was the eye, suspending what it saw in what it still sees, where there was nothing left to see. From where I stood it was plain I must let my answer be either yes or no, though I had only half a mind to answer. The other half was hung up on an oath taking hold—a little longer, a bit more—with the windfalls at my feet and the sky emptying out before me. Would that I could bring the body down, beneath the slow winter wasps and the tree withstanding its mutilations. Between the late sun, thief of shadows, and the morning sun, for whom the river would not part. I would say fall on us, green mountains. I would say cover us, green hills.

THE ACCIDENTAL

The end of a thing is the term of its appetite.

—ST THOMAS AQUINAS

"Father, they killed us."

—JUAN RULFO

And when the soul saw the father in the yard with his water hose spraying the widows from the eaves, it paused to smell the water warming on the smooth cement, for it was summer, and night, and in the porchlight the widows legged their shadows into the rough shingles of the house where the water formed droplets and the eaves dripped with light. The soul breathed in and filled itself with the father's water and the father's widows, and tied itself off with a tether as the hose ran from the spigot into the father's hand, and poured itself into the widows corners and into the earholes in the cement exhaling their pockets of air, and it yanked and rankled where its skin puckered closed at the end of its line, and it filled with the father and grew taut and thin-skinned until it developed a luster, a smooth reflecting sheen just apparent in the porch light among the widows' spindling in the shadows and the droplets falling from the shingles and the moths pressed flat against the fixture. Thus, it attached itself to its reflection so as to remain visible.

So, though the soul could not see itself, it thought itself in sight. It thought itself thinking itself dream and dreamed itself am. But the thought of the sight of itself in daylight made it ache with doubt. For it was dark. Inside and out, what it was was obscure. So it opened a hole in its garment and found skin. It opened a hole in its skin and found lips at the mouth of it. It opened its lips. It heaved a plain saline bile into the sod at its feet and trembled, for there was pain, revulsion, a shock of sun caught in the strings of clear mucus that hung between blades of grass in gorgeous syncretic arcs (—& therein, suspension, passage, time: the hanged man's arrested embrace—) which the soul then admired as its own work until the wind lit through the blades and spattered the ants roiling in the roots. The green spring wept out of it, the sun's darting glance through the wound's lips in the skin went out of it. It wept itself inside out, and the soul saw that it saw through the wound.

The wound was a source. A question. And the question was not the wound's hole but the hole the wound makes in the skin everywhere it looks: are you an it . . . ? is it a you . . . ? —and these were the everywhere wounds in the whole which were else, other than the soul. Though at first the difference between who and what was no difference. At first there was always likeness, always the face in the surface, all a sort of you. The clover thrust its round shoulders through the grass while the soul rested on its belly and felt the cool sweet skin of leaves on its new lips. The soul's mouth was wet. The earth was wet. The faces in the clover pinched their mouths up to receive the bees and the bees wobbled gladly. The mouths gazed at the soul from their eyeless crowns and the soul gazed back with its open mouth where it kept them. At first it put everything in the bed of its mouth where the question was, for this was love.

And when the father's pickup steered into the pall of dust and began to disappear, the soul, losing heart, followed after. They trailed the riverbed to where the father pulled driftwood knots from a bend in the banks of dry sand. *A marionette, a paintbrush holder, a snake in a nest of birds, a harmonica for Christopher,* the father making discoveries, his eyes in the torques of wood, his hands testing for brittleness and rot where the nails would fail, and the soul pressed its lips into the hollows, feeling itself warm there like a flame in the grain. It pined into the loose bark which the father stripped from the joints and fed to the braised fish on his kindling fire. It writhed in the blaze with a figure like a four-sided man, which the father would later carve out from memory, according to the beauty of a four-sided man, and which he would hold up to scrutiny by the dark oil of the lamps that cast their apocrypha across his workbench at home.

While love was made in likeness, the question grew. Before it choked to a close for all it liked, it swallowed whole fingers pressed to its lips, a fist inside, a wrist to the elbow, to probe for the dream. At last, reaching through disbelief it forced the rood of its own limb into the depths of the cleft, and there it held itself open, and there it waited, impaled on extremities, and was plunged. So, it was the wounded rooted around in the wounded looking for a portrait. It was like reaching into reflection, the river rippling into glass that shook to pieces overhanging trees and sky. It was like listening for avowals in the echoes from the cliffs: five thousand yawned open. How could they all be fed? The shallows shivered in the breeze, the soul lost sight of its reflection, and the minnows nipped and prattled at a bottom feeder snagged on a fisher's lost spoon. Entrails, gill skin, waved in the current like a shroud and the minnows plunked mouthfuls from the mute flesh. Their mouths made a sound as they broke the surface, a puncture, then a gasp, and the soul thought: this is the sound for hunger.

Then the soul lost sight of the father, too. The soul turning its wound to the horizon where the fire was no longer visible. The soul turning inward, wanting. Thus, when loneliness took root it grew limbs. It grew a tensile, nervous lattice of branches racing into the cavity at the center of its head, under its skin, into its cranium and eyes, so that through the brambles shuddering in its crown, the soul saw something of itself with its own eyes turned inward: eyes for the picking, clustered like cherries. And as the soul's eyes filled with lust for more visions, more eyes plumped into being. A mass of capillaries seized in the mouth of the question, cutting teeth in all the mouths at the heart of it, and each had a sound for what it closed on, uniform though incredulous: here I am. It was the sound of a feast. Startled aloud, the owls rose up with wings and a furl of calls from their roosts on the crags. The soul plucked pulp from the thorns, brought it through the brambles, brought it witting to its mouth: *I am who that is who.*

So how is it done: the I seeking itself in itself where what is already finished requires finishing, the I determined in its I to bring the I forth in its own regard and without sacrifice. The I in conception, in realization, in equation. The two symmetrical halves of its head spiraling east and west into the thicket, the head ramming its way into the midst by the horns, by the haunches, where sinews divide into sinews and mount the bones and bind them—tooth to jaw, eye to socket, articulation to articulation, contracting. The ribs on either side thrust their panoply from the spine and met in the middle around the heart, and the spine held the head alert while the head willed the spine to hoof it forward, and the spine did, shoulders, hamstrings, heaving behind the coiled head which way it turned, though the head stuck fast behind the eyes rolling in the skull, though the eyes held fast to the wool of the thicket, it would.

[—& therein: suspension, being, passage, time: midway in the wood of myself, the lost wills lumbered together. Between the hemisphere of the I othering itself—me—& the hemisphere of the I woulding other as itself—you—that was the law. It seemed will would discover no other. To become the sole subject of the law that would secure an image of the law & that would raise the image into practice (—self as monument, vessel, frame, orb, boundary, mechanism, volume, crux—) & to practice exaltation of the image in the name of the law & to keep the haven of the law's name-minded end, which is none other than to make something real of the would of myself before me & to take leave & leaves of me, artfully . . .]

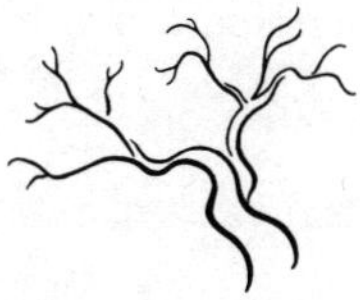

All the faint rasping sounds together became a breath. The felt animal in the infant's bed whispered in the infant's grasp. Rasp of the foam pearls inside the faux fur. Lack coinciding with touch. What did it want? Wholeness & the illusion of wholeness, forever. So, the infant gave & gave over, grasping the felt body which held what the infant felt. Animal of pearls, wake of pearls foaming into the hollow of the arm, the neck & joints, the chest. Hollows the will fills in the difference between the stuffed animal & the stuffed infant, the thing held off by the secret inside the felt thing, the rasp that spoke at the touch, one tiny body against another tiny body, but that never spoke at all.

Cottonwoods, river. Black bull. When the animal rose from the water, a dark hole bloomed in the center of the shallows. The child halted fast in its tracks & the child's reflection—watching what it watched, remembering what it remembered—doubled & redoubled the image of the child's body wavering, flaring, in the pools. The animal brooded in its selfsame shadow, the pools shivered & seized in the breeze, & the cottonwoods broke & snowed across the surface that foiled & bent its trees inward. Beautiful, the flurries of seed in sunlight, air, river. Beautiful, the scene filling with white snow that screened the glittering leaves, & the flaming mirrors of the pools, & the oily shadow that trickled into the flames & spread. The animal stood over it, motionless, limbs & tail trailing the length of the pools, its hide so dark it seemed entire eye & mouth. It stared, hidden in plain view. The seed mothed softly everywhere. It made a white pelt of the face of the pools & a white light of rebounding shadow. Everything happened twice in this opening—as wonder, as terror—then transpired again. The tree seed fell. The animal drank in the river, & a river flowed out of it. Beyond this, there seemed no territory.

Rain falls in the mind, assorted & inexact, drop-locked, rolling where it might, whole lochs bearing monsters from the slightest divots & pouring mostly beyond knowing. So that a detail fleshes an art. So that any species is possible. The taxidermist strokes the velvet moss of his whale's bones & sees antlers. Or a set of wrists. To handcuff. To set in stillness as a statue. To set in flight as a feathered thing in a window box. To face a God. The taxidermist remembers the kind of eyes. He sets his glass into the hide & looks for an expression to emerge. The child watches the rain make idle prisms on the lace curtains that write their silhouettes across the lifelike forms that hang from the taxidermist's walls. The child knows error enters here. But the child cannot look away.

Our father brought home stone & words for stone: blue azurite, yellow agate, green malachite, pink granite, iron pyrite, gray flint. He brought home history in stone: fool's gold, slag, pottery shards, geodes, turquoise beads, window panes made from mica, arrowheads carved from obsidian, & fossils of inscrutable shape left behind by an old sea. He brought home truckloads of earth to run through his sluice box & he panned for gold flakes that he stored in distilled water in a clear glass vial. He made magnets to sort iron filings from the sawdust on his workshop floor. He melted iron & gold into ring-shaped molds he chiseled from river stone. He tumbled rock smooth to polish tiger's eye for his pocket. He brought home graphite pencils numbered in gradations of hardness & darkness & he kept his pencils sharpened to the quick & ordered in a wooden drawer. He made paints from ground minerals & linseed oil. He fired riverbank clay with grass to make brick. He brought home watercolors & brushes & gum erasers & tracing paper with tiny grids & at night he penciled tiny decimals into his gridded books while gazing through his scope at the moon. He photographed star trails & orbiting planets & he practiced mirror-writing with his sinister hand. He measured rain & acid levels in rain, in dirt. He walked the radius of the mine, diviner of pipe lines & ore lines & shaft lines from the palimpsests of the maw's previous lives. He made maps of basins & elevations. He made maps of weather & night skies. He made dove calls to summon doves & fish lures to summon fish. To summon the right words—fair words, white words, bright words—he made a box.

World-Making: Foundations of a Marvelous Science

I

A phantom touch, & the dreamer folded on its lungs & dragged its good half leftward, heart over foot, wheezing & shamed. The phantom mouths blew & blinded the dreamer & spun it on its foot like a weathercock, westward, the dreamer thrown towards the college enclosed by low stone walls, the dreamer thrown against the chapel's sealed iron doors. Someone stepped into the path & walked past. Someone else addressed the dreamer by name with a message: *Señor has something for you.* All the people around sat on the still grass. There was a baby with heat rash asleep in a stroller, his mother fanning & beaming at a man with wet armpits who coddled his buckle while he talked. There was a sweaty-headed boy bent over a book. The pretzel man stood by his wagon & counted money in the shade of his wilting yellow umbrella. The dreamer spun counterclockwise & slumped useless on its heart & fought to walk upright & fought to catch its breath. Someone held out a hand cupping a round little thing, a strange melon or a nut or a tiny brain furrowing into itself. Thing so small it could hardly exist without falling into nothing. The dreamer, calmed now, gazed at it & wondered what can this be? *Everything that is made,* wonder said. & the phantom mouths blew, & the round little thing made out to be nothing, & the soul, itself nothing, could not decide.

II

What remained to be touched? Not the poor room's woodstove waving with ash. Not the flickering hole among mountains & clouds where the dreamer hid its face as the wind departed, leaving air enough for fire. Fire at the mouth. Mouth down the mountain licks tender into the folds of the valley, valley mouthing fire into sand, sand mouthing desert into fire. The dreamer in the hole hid its head in the dark as the fire departed, leaving sheer rock & trembling. Trembling, the shadows beat their wings against the walls & crept downward into shadow, & the rock face shuddered & the rock face shuddered, and the dreamer seized its face in the folds of its garment as the beating departed with night in the wake, and lightning. Night, the blown mountains; night & the valley of sand; night & the flickering roots of the missing trees that dead-end in rock; night, the graves, the flash of bones, the thunder jaws the air. The dreamer hid its face in its hands. The thunder spoke, and the bones rose and came together, bone to bone, upright, strapped with gristle & muscle, sacked in fat & skin, and there was night, adoring bone adoring bone. The sleepers stared into the burden of the valley of dream, and the dreamer walked among them & hid among them, the legion thunder, the bodies blousing in wind.

III

Where was the evangelist but fording upriver with objects in either of his outstretched hands, the book in his mouth fluttering with breath?

If it is not the automaton
in reach, not the chirruping box
wired to the grinding handle, its
hairlike filaments & almost
human voices & sky-high bills
tuned to feeds & ink, & if not
the snapshoot dial of the eye,
& hinged exteriors & microflight
iMind refresh cells, & if never
again real demons, no, but those
modified, fractal, in the pools; it
is the make-believe shell
tunneling forever in itself. It is
retrieving its own pearl. It paves
a deepening hollow as it goes. It
spills iridescent passages that
envelop the river in reflections
& light, yes. & finless, they
flood the shores with their lore,
& warm their scales, their
extravagant blue-green golden
tails, on the banks & sing.

The evangelist lunged between river & sky, river-sky expanding, contracting, in the scene, the motion of the evangelist a still point in the meeting between water & air. Lung of the sky: drifting circumference. Lung of the river: black vein of the sea wrings the sea. But as the day rolled away, the rim of the world approached headlong, & a rift wavered faintly around. A line, was it? A decision taking hold, mirror-like, I think, & vain? The evangelist, hardly visible now, more dream than prophet, became a figure moving through the swaying poppy fields. & the book, still fluttering, became a figure of sleep. Lung of the sky, sheer old ghost. Lung of the river, strong brown god. & the dream let the matter drop. And the book flapped apart by halves & halves. & the last of the book fell away.

The Wall

Where shall I exit & how? From leaves become stone, from riverbed stones in the walls around trees? If you are able. By expulsion through a sieve? Never to return? This also. Looking back, the sieve shook violently, & the soul passed through as though passing through itself. But it arrived as though arriving at some other. One which sought the tree within the leaves as it watched the leaves & shook. Which fell as the leaves fell from the tree to the sieves of the earth & made stone. The leaves, which helixed their vegetable ladders through the layered weight of all the earth & limned their widowed ghosts into mineral cells. The leaves, which writ their veins in stone. The stones, which wore their leaves in water down to wall-sized loaves. The stones, so many minds set & in their own way. The soul, who held each stone as leaves in the sieve. Who set each stone as leaves in the wall. The wall, which hungered to begin again, and which reached for the drop at the end of the earth & built itself & grew. As did the railroad track, the highway, & the bridge. & the wall crossed them all. & sleep, which closed its eye to the wall & overwhelmed the earth & its animals, which is its purpose.

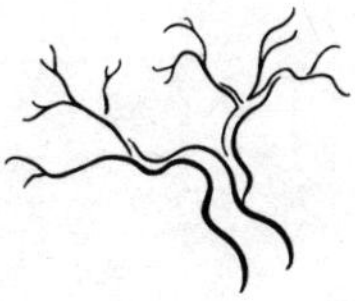

The child ran about absorbed in life, quiet, full of amusement. She did not notice things, nor changes nor alterations. One day she would find daisies in the grass, another day, apple-blossoms would be sprinkled white on the ground, and she would run among it, for pleasure because it was there. Yet again birds would be pecking at the cherries, her father would throw cherries down from the tree all round her on the garden. Then the fields were full of hay.

She did not remember what had been nor what would be, the outside things were there each day. She was always herself, the world outside was accidental. Even her mother was accidental to her: a condition that happened to endure.

—D.H. LAWRENCE, *The Rainbow*

The Spirit Is Blood from a Stone

To bed, I guess, that weary enough I can erase
for a night those accidents of spirit and flesh
who amuse themselves by bringing the lynch mob
behind me—whose old glittering eyes have made me
a guest in my mother's house, an orphan, an illiterate,
and a law-abiding whore. In whose eyes I find
my brother again, and dream him among the order
of fathers whose work made a desert of me, just as I
worked to desert them in the desert, rock picks
in their belts, the shade of their hats against miles of sand
that dazzle the mind with the tracks of those who
followed too, mulish, towards veins of metal running
through the land up north, so rich, the mother lode,
you can dig it out with a spoon, so certain that bolas
de plata some four thousand pounds were found
even after the days Francisco Vázquez de Coronado
went seeking the cities of legend for God and gold.
Granted, the expedition of fourteen hundred men
and fifteen hundred animals did not find the riches
of which they had been told. They arrived
in this country with swords and the pope when shovels
and prayer have profited better on the wayside, as it goes,
lined with the sun-bleached bones of unfortunate men.
The earth did not devour them, much as they compassed,
all their days—what a thing to do—to eat dust. Going
south and further south, I saw the adits carved

into the high red cliffs. They mouth the gritty attending
silence of the Coronado Trail. I did not understand.

Consider: salt of the earth, sulfur, rain, copper, air,
rolling down in drops, seeping into the mineshafts,
bubbling, hissing in the limestone, weeping tears
over tears, following slow, indiscernible, involuntary,
relentless—it trails from the walls, eats with abandon,
rains. It makes its way in the dark, its crystalline habits,
its metallic and sweet taste, its incomprehensible electric
blue, so blue the gamblers carry it for luck and the women
say it protects against el ojo; a necessary evil,
this bluestone, Roman vitriol, blue copperas, chalcanthite,
copper sulfate, all the makings of a caustic beginning.
One thing is clear: blue water means copper, a lot of it,
resting just below the iron-red soil you see driving down
route 666 into town past Cole's Pizza and the schoolyard,
the dealership, Maud's, the courthouse where I carved
my name into the old soft brick, and the river whose
hundred-year floods would bring my father to hang
St. Christopher around his neck, to call his son,
my brother, by the name of one so surely cast out
even the nomadic children of the sun might be
lifted up and carried from one turn to another
in his hands, as the river turns water. Be patient,
my love, I am telling you: in the crossing the light

breaks you, hailing, dying in cries, praising you
among tongues like white wings darting on the surface,
and below, where moss pulls at your legs, entrails
of legions who have sworn themselves over to guard
your will against your will, say yes, indefinitely, here you
are at last, but where you thought you could get to
is not for you to end. What did you think?
That the whole would unfold at once in a breath, in birth,
this child at home, cast out, whose task in this world
is to carry you in his chest, behind his ribs, you,
pouring in, out, of the two halves of his heart?

I kept you wandering through the mazes
of the underground mines, far below the roots of the shrubs,
where blue water seeps through the shafts and bluestone
gathers in the veins. Against my will and yours, I held
the considerable weight of you in my hands. I dig
you up, find you watering the small swelling lawn, unearth
you in front of the little green-shingled company house
weeding a trellis of pink roses by the door and the cactus
you planted in the flowerbeds. You rake, dig into rock
and clay, break clods of earth in your hands, plant
seeds you buy at the company store. You hum
through copper wires running through my house.
I would have walked the earth without the earth
you walked—I would not have looked back—backbone, stone,
what are they doing now but looking up

from their work towards the sky, Díos mío,
in the east and the north, just beyond
the next border?—had you not decreed my silence.

Wise up, güerita. Spanish wasn't allowed.
Forced at gunpoint into cattle boxes, deported
to New Mexico, left in the desert. Communists,
enemy aliens, obstructing production in a time
of war. We strike. We await contracts with hands
at our brothers' throats. Walk the earth if you will,
since you will not find shelter in your father's
company—this much I promise—for that mouth.

It is unfortunate. Perhaps you would like to negotiate
the terms of the impasse (who would notice it).
Bear in mind: we wish to state one conclusion
with all the emphasis at our command. Every day
this difference is prolonged constitutes a threat
to our general welfare. We realize the stakes
are high. We understand why you have found it
difficult to reach an agreement. It is the nation itself,
however, which here has most at stake. No loss can
compare with what the country between you suffers.

Backcountry, wading next to you in the green pools
of the river. We bake fish on hot stones beside our fire,
watch the cliffs for bighorn scaling the rock

above us. Downstream, where the figs grow wild
we make our way to the abandoned mineshaft,
our destination. The bats have taken over
and the stench of their droppings stops us even as
the cavernous heart, so old, so difficult, pauses, is
silenced, sleeps by us patiently, even as
we are silenced in my memory of us transfixed
in its eye. We've come all this way to our ruin: all
but in our having known it, vanished.

NOTES

This section's two epigraphs come from the following sources:

Simone Weil, "Illusions," *Gravity and Grace,* translated by Emma Crawford and Mario von der Ruhr, Routledge, 1999.

Juan Rulfo, "They gave us the land," *The Burning Plain and Other Stories,* translated by George D. Schade, University of Texas Press, 2001.

"Otherwise All Would Be God" was originally published with the following note, and refers to the two sources listed below:

The title of this poem is taken from Simone Weil's "Decreation." Elsewhere, in her final letter to Father Perrin, Weil writes, "I never read the story of the barren fig tree without trembling. I think that it is a portrait of me. In it also, nature was powerless, and yet it was not excused." The poem was written several years after my maternal grandmother's death in the 1998 flood of Del Rio, Texas and Ciudad Acuña, Mexico. Her body washed out of her house, down her street, and was caught in a dead tree, which thankfully allowed her body to be found. The poem is about my last visit to the tree.

Simone Weil, "Decreation," *Gravity and Grace,* Routledge, 1999.

Simone Weil, "Last Thoughts," *Waiting for God,* translated by Emma Crawford, Harper & Row, 1973.

Substantial

This section's epigraph is taken from Simone Weil, "The Cross," *Gravity and Grace,* Routledge, 1999.

"The Stone Is Worldless" quotes from Sirach 27:4 in the italicized language in the parentheses. The epigraph is from a section title in Martin Heidegger's *The Fundamental Concepts of Metaphysics,* translated by William McNeill and Nicholas Walker, Indiana University Press, 1995 (Part One, Chapter Two, Section 23.d). The title of the poem is from the same work (Part Two, Chapter Two, Section 42). In this section, Heidegger formulates a three-part thesis: the stone has no world, the animal is world-poor, and human beings are world-making.

"Fiat" is a response to Dante Gabriel Rossetti's painting of the Annunciation, *Ecce Ancilla Domini!*

"What Shall I Cry" takes its title and epigraph from Isaiah 40:6.

"The Animal Is Poor in the World" takes its title from Martin Heidegger's *The Fundamental Concepts of Metaphysics,* Indiana University Press, 1995 (Part Two, Chapter Two, Section 42).

"The Line" takes its epigraph from refusingtoforget.org and closes with references to Matthew 5:37 and John 20:13–15. The poem is based on various historical accounts of mob violence against Mexicans and Mexican Americans, particularly along the Mexico–Texas border. The poem also references the violence that took place during the Arizona mine strike of 1983. For more contexts, see monroeworktoday.org, an extension of Monroe Work's archive, which attempts to map white supremacy mob violence against individuals from nonwhite groups, including people identified as Chinese, black, Italian, Latin@, and Native American. See also Jonathan D. Rosenblum's *Copper Crucible: How the Arizona Miners' Strike of 1983 Recast Labor-Management Relations in America,* Cornell University ILR Press, 1998.

"The Spirit Is Bone" takes its title from G. W. F. Hegel's *Phenomenology of Spirit,* translated by A. V. Miller, Oxford University Press, 1977 (Part C. (AA.) Reason: Section c. Observation of self-consciousness in its relation to its immediate actuality. Physiognomy and Phrenology).

"Refrain" takes its epigraph from Martin Heidegger's *The Fundamental Concepts of Metaphysics,* Indiana University Press, 1995 (Part Two, Chapter Two, Section 42).

"Substantial" opens with language that alludes to John Ashbery's "The New Spirit," *Three Poems*, The Viking Press, 1972.

"Water in Water" takes its title and epigraph from Georges Bataille's "Animality," in *Theory of Religion*, translated by Robert Hurley, Zone Books, 1992.

"Annunciation of the Self-Enclosed God" takes its title from G. W. F. Hegel, *Lectures on the Philosophy of Religion, Volume I,* Peter C. Hodgson, Editor, translated by R. F. Brown, P. C. Hodgson, and J. M. Stewart, University of California Press, 1984 (Part I, "Lectures of 1827: A. The Concept of God"). The italicized language at the end of the poem is from Song of Solomon 7:12–13.

"The Spirit is Thrown" takes its epigraph from Martin Heidegger, *Being and Time,* translated by Joan Stambaugh, State University of New York Press, 2010 (Part One, Division Two, Chapter Two, 58).

"Retablo:" opens with language that alludes to Wallace Stevens's "Owls Clover," *Wallace Stevens: Collected Poetry and Prose,* The Library of America, 1997.

"Our Mother of Rivers is Made Our Perpetual Hanging Garden" is for Carmen Rios—my maternal grandmother who drowned in the 1998 flooding of the San Felipe neighborhoods of Del Rio, Texas—whose grave still lacks a stone. The close of the poem references Matthew 5:37 and Luke 23:30.

The Accidental

Epigraphs for this section are taken from the following sources:

Saint Thomas Aquinas, *The Summa Contra Gentiles of Saint Thomas Aquinas: Volume Three, Part I,* Chapter XVI, "That the End of Everything is a Good," translated by the English Dominican Fathers, Burn Oates & Washbourne LTD, Imprimatur 1928.

Juan Rulfo, "Paso del Norte," *The Burning Plain and Other Stories,* translated by George D. Schade, University of Texas Press, 2001.

"World Making: Foundations of a Marvelous Science" first appeared in publication with an epigraph: "Three dreams and modernity appear in the scene, hand in hand with misgiving: November 10, 1619." René Descartes used the term, "mirabilis sientiae fundamenta"—"foundations of a marvelous science"—to describe his philosophy. The poem is based on an account of three dreams that Descartes had on the night of November 10, 1619. See Stephen Gaukroger's *Descartes: An Intellectual Biography,* Oxford University Clarendon Press, 1997. The concept, "world-forming," is from Martin Heidegger's *The Fundamental Concepts of Metaphysics*, Indiana University Press, 1995 (Part Two, Chapter Two, Section 42).

The final section's epigraph is taken from D. H. Lawrence, *The Rainbow*, "The Child," Random House: The Modern Library, 1915.

"The Spirit is Blood from a Stone" first appeared in publication with an epigraph: "I have known several who came back from there who now amuse themselves by talking of how it would be to go back and proceed to recover that which is lost, while others enjoy trying to find the reason why it was discovered at all." See *The Journey of Coronado 1540–1542: from the City of Mexico to the Grand Canyon of the Colorado and the Buffalo Plains of Texas, Kansas, and Nebraska*, translated by George Parker Winship, A. S. Barnes & Company, 1904. The poem is an elegy for Charles "Charlie" B. Franco, interred Carlos Bustamante Franco, third-generation copper miner, my father. His grave also lacks a stone.